~ *Ventricular Soliloquies* ~
By
Haneef Sabree

COPYRIGHT© 2013 BY HANEEF SABREE

ALL RIGHTS RESERVED. NO PART OF THIS BOOK MAY BE REPRODUCED, STORED IN A RETRIEVAL SYSTEM, OR TRANSMITTED BY ANY MEANS WITHOUT THE EXPRESSED WRITTEN PERMISSION OF THE AUTHOR.

FIRST PRINTING: 2013

COVER DESIGN: Mike "Will" Wright

GRAPHIC DESIGNER: SOS Graphic Design Co.

EDITOR: Haneef Sabree

AUTHOR PHOTOGRAPH: Timothy Paule

PUBLISHED BY YOUNG BREED PUBLICATIONS
INKSTER, MI 48141

EMAIL: hjsabree@att.net

WEBSITE: www.hjsabree.wix.com/jrhandsonsllc

LIBRARY OF CONGRESS CONTROL NUMBER: 2013912011

ISBN: 978-0-9846633-0-9 (pbk.)

About the Author

- Second literary work
- Sophomore publication proceeded by "Trumping a Fixed Deck"
- Entrepreneur, educator, humanitarian and youth advocate
- A product of the illustrious HBCU, Philander Smith College, class of 02'
- This collection of poems is embedded in imagery, synergy and authenticity. "Ventricular Soliloquies" is a rare, engaging and innovative account.

Did You Know?

- Is a graduate of Inkster High School from the unforgettable class of 96'
- Won 1st place in the first ever district wide Science Fair, (project on electromagnetism) representing Meek Elementary School in 1987
- Sister Clara Muhammad School in Detroit, MI (formerly on Van Dyke off 94) provided the author with the best educational experience, second to none.
- "Instead of Tears" was dedicated to his long time classmate & friend Toni Battle
- Met Sister Afeni Shakur, mother of the late Tupac Shakur, at the Truth Bookstore in Northland Mall (Southfield, MI); the occasion was a book signing for the release of Sister Afeni's new book at the time, " The Evolution of a Revolutionary."
- His cousin DJ Sweetz is considered one of the best DJs in the state of Michigan.

The Baobab Tree: Knowledge & Life

"Life without knowledge is death in disguise."
                                          -Talib Kweli

"Whatever a believer attempts to do, he/she seeks to perfect it."
                                          –The Holy Quran

"The more you know, is when you realize how much you don't know."
                                          –Unknown

"Knowledge is power, and power is key to changing things."
                                          –Jill Nelson

"Mansions, cars, property, money in the bank can create an environment conducive for happiness but cannot give happiness in themselves."
                                          -Anonymous

Why were we given two ears and one mouth?....

Dedicated to: the spirit-lifters, fallen generals and all those who work hard each and every day and never get their pay nor the recognition they so rightfully deserve.

Table of Contents

Ponderable Cognitions of a General..ix
Sunshine..xi

SOLILOQUIES

Roads That Turn..2
Seventh Heaven..3
Timeless Confessions..4
Undying Flame..5
Untitled 2...6
Untitled 6...7
Wife Material..8
Imprints...9
Words Get N the Way..12
You Say U R My Friend..13
Your Heart, My World..14
2 Win Back Your Heart..15
A Letter 4 the Sistas..16
Ain't No Luv 4 a Nigga...17
Briitist Daye..18
The Price Ain't Rite...19
2 ∞..20
Celebratin' the Queens of the Earth..21
I Know I'm Somebody...22
Proverbial Interlude..23
The Dragon Tale...25
Sabreeisms..26
Mental Salvation..27
Custom Made...28
Fever of Luv...29
If I Ever..30
Lil' Miss Cutie Pie...31
Mirage, My Queen..32
No Distance Between...33
Dowhn4mifamilee...34

West Memphis 35
Sorri Littlle Coloured Boye 36
What is Beautiful? 38
That Ain't Gangsta 39
Lifzrime 40
My Main Man 41
Hilton's Palace 42

INTANGIBLES
Distinguished Establishments 45
Music & Movie Classicz 46
Sitcoms & Recommended Websites 47
Reading List 48

BONUS
Buster Free 50
Dancinawfbeet 51
The Reboh 52

21 GUN SALUTE
Medals of Honor 54
Acknowledgments 55
Agenda 56
Initiatives Part I & II 58
Words of Wisdom 64

SOLILOQUIES BY BRO. DENNIS SABREE
Untitled verses 65

EMPTY THE WHOLE CLIP
City Council 74
My Brother D 75
That's My D.O.A.E.D.D^2.I 76
Taking It 2 the Rack 78

Ponderable Cognitions of a General

No king or queen is meant to be confined. What "they" don't conceptualize or care to conceptualize is that truth sooner or later will prevail. For it was written. Suppressive and unruly systems or people are destined to fall.

For the youth:

My young brothers and sisters take time to analyze and come to grips with your supreme worth and value. As African Americans for instance, we don't understand our worth; we have the power to shut down Wall Street, public transit systems in any state, business, or even America if we only knew. The dope game is not what you might think it is; the end results of a life comprised of drug selling, drug using or the in-between is either the grave or prison, point blank. It's imperative that you learn how to resolve conflict and your differences without resorting to physical aggression (so often). The law and other organizations of servitude have long pointed their guns and artillery at you as the main target, not Israel, Pakistan or China for example. By the former, that means watch your associations, develop your skill sets, be a leader not a follower, listen to the ones that care about you and if something sounds too good to be true, recognize it probably is.

To the middle age:

We have to set a better example for the youth, because leaders require leadership. Someone has to step up and break the vicious cycle resulting in our children having no positive male role models (this doesn't have to be fulfilled biologically), broken homes and the fallacy of doing as I say not as I do. It's important that a concerted effort is put forth, by individuals who are middle-aged to help bridge the gap between the elders and the young. We have to take back our communities by organization and implementation; for example bringing the football, basketball and baseball leagues back for the children, tapping into the fields of agriculture and skilled trades more proactively and strategically. At the end of the day internalize the fact that big problems don't necessarily require complex solutions.

For the elders:

You represent the eyes and backbone of the community. The youth will never respect you if the respect doesn't come with reciprocity. Instead of criticizing and condemning the youth on so many levels, a more effective approach would be to reach out and help them. For instance, you could reach out by getting more involved in community-based functions or Big Brother and Big Sister type programs. Religious institutions have to extend the message of spirituality beyond the four walls of congregation. The last two points include the middle-age group as well. In order to shift the paradigm so that it is right-side up will require the assemblage of all three age groups to some degree; bear in mind that it's best to start small and build from there. Because as we all know, Rome wasn't built overnight. It has been done before; thus anything that has been done in the past carries feasibility for being cultivated into fruition in regards to the present and future.

Soliloquies

Roads That Turn

I told her I loved her,

Did she believe what I said,

I learned a long time ago,

That it consist of more,

Than just hittin' the bed,

I've held on so true,

With no hesitation about stickin' it thru,

But its all cool,

Cause I meant what I said,

When I told her I luv u,

The hardest thing 4 me,

Is forgiveness,

But I did that 2,

Before me,

I look out 4 u,

Will I be used like a tool,

Does she see me as,

The joker's fool,

Infinite luv requires 2.

Seventh Heaven

Built as a goddess,

Threshold 4 pain & perseverance,

Is far beyond us,

If u represented a number,

It would have 2 b seven,

Cause the totality of your endowments,

Had 2 extend str8 from heaven,

Femininity 2nd to none,

More potent & respected,

Than the blast from a military gun,

I must testify,

Your gifts are truly a blessin',

Like the energy from the sun.

Timeless Confessions

I can't control how I feel,

But what I know is,

The feelings are real,

My drive is triggered by your total self,

& your priceless wealth,

Not solely on your sex appeal,

Your complete package is the golden seal,

I miss the talks,

I look forward to us strolling down the board walk,

As we exchange thoughts,

N a way that makes time appear still,

Seeing u holding down the fort,

Gives me such a thrill,

Maintaining the family, job, & school,

Amongst the many other things u do,

Propels me 2 give madd props 2 u,

Had 2 let u know I was thinking about u,

Had 2 let u know I appreciate the resilient strong black woman n u,

My inspirations & psyche toward u,

Above anything else,

Is pure & incontrovertibly all so true.

Undying Flame

If I could do it all over again,
I would make sure,
B4 we became lovers,
We were friends,
I don't want our camaraderie 2 eva terminally descend,
Thru mistakes and lack of experience,
I have influenced your outlook 2 bend,
My motivation is 2 make it str8 again,
2 invigorate your smile and happiness,
So genuine,
When we can no longer c the light at the end,
That's when faith kicks n,
Being with u,
Is a double win,
So much on my mind,
Focus resides,
N cultivating the bond 2 ascend,
My motive flows rhythmically,
From within,
being the man your spirit would commend,
the fire I have 4 u,
has no beginning,
nor an end.

Untitled 2

When u have 2 go,

That's why n my mind I say stay,

Makin' luv 2 u,

Is hard hittin',

With the potency of Tangueray,

4 eva my superstar,

With u it feels better than,

The best of wins,

(or having a million dollars 2 spend),

I won't stop until 1 day u say,

"Damn Baby!,"

U r a 10.

Untitled 6

When things fall apart,

Keep this close 2 your heart,

Because it's quite obvious,

You've been an elegant Queen,

From the start.

Wife Material

I've come across a legion of women,

But none were on the same level as u,

Their love was insipid and Teflon,

Sicker than any flu,

When provisos became difficult & trying,

The rest of them were fluctuant,

and abandoned ship or split,

"But your devotion?,"

Picture an Alaskan Malamutes' fur,

Is husky,

Rather vastly thick,

U cannot be categorized,

As merely a homegyrl, consort, or friend,

4 u r authenticated as,

Wife material.

Imprints

Hilton Jones

Left to Right:
Aunt Cheryl
and Uncle Andrew

Left to Right:
Dolores Sabree (Mom),
Leslie, Aunt Ruthie and C.J.

Left to Right:
Leslie and
Aunt Ruthie

Uncle Jim, Dolores Sabree (mom) & Dennis Sabree (dad)

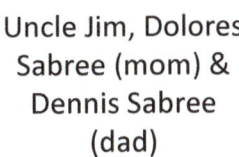

Hawaii 1996 – Mental Therapy

Words Get N the Way

U never get a second chance,

To make a 1st impression,

U fulfilled that without any questions,

When I chill with you,

 I have no need to be stressin',

I look forward to our sessions,

Your mind, body, & total self is a blessing,

Forget a second helping,

Cause that's not enough,

So much to say,

Sometimes words could never convey.

You Say U R My Friend

During vicious times and days so cold,

My homeyz are there,

Quite quick and bold,

In the faces of defeat or even death,

They're in the struggle,

Til' there's nothing left,

Always keeping it on the up & up,

Not playing themselves,

Fighting against the grind,

Not blaming anyone else,

Giving props where credits due,

Without the thought,

 of ever vilifying as if a plastic dude,

if you can truly say I gave it my all,

then finding strength in each other should be there when one starts to fall.

Your Heart, My World

So many places 2 begin,

At first,

All I wanted 2 b was a friend,

But that soon came 2 an end,

Your role exceeds the boundaries of just a partisan,

Never meant 2 appear stingy,

But my love 4 u is graphic,

As if a shark frenzy,

Being dedicated + committed,

Is just the soulja n me.

It appears questions have been raised,

Wasn't tryin' 2 put the relationship n a maze,

I take full responsibility 4 any mistakes that I made,

It's u & only u that I crave,

Your heart,

I must save,

I put that on my grave,

4eva a part of me as if engraved,

Willing 2 do whatever's necessary,

2 make sure that foundation is laid.

2 Win Back Your Heart

My plan is to win back your heart,

Like it was from the start,

If I fail or come up short,

At least I would have tried tirelessly,

2 do my part,

Never dreamed of causing u any distress or shame,

My aim,

Is to provide 4 u a covenant,

Against the pouring rain,

2 make u smile & happy,

Again and again,

2 show u the world,

& embrace u with riches,

U so rightfully deserve,

2 do the little things,

Which mean so much,

2 leave your fine, fine self,

N a permanent blush,

We don't have 2 rush,

We don't have 2 fuss,

Can't stand 2 c u stressed so much,

baby you are such a plus,

That's why I'll do my part,

2 win back your heart.

A Letter 4 the Sistas

U stay racing in my mind,
I c vivid pictures of u,
Because you're fine as wine,
When we chill,
Feels like we spark an internal shine,
& I want you all the time,
I look forward to the convo,
Cause baby you ease & comfort my mind,
I had 2 put u Ms. Sexy,
In this rhyme,
Just like seeing 'The Big Dipper' or 'Haley's Comet',
Babygirl you're once in a lifetime,
U illuminate as if a diamond,
In full effect -- sublime,
You'll never o.d. from the pressure,
I won't let ya',
Instead I'm a catch ya',
Then wet ya',
With kisses from the soul,
Spending moments with u,
Is what I'm anticipatin',
Skip the dough,
You're the type of woman,
I've been missin',
2 make a soulja become whole,
Your body & mind moves me,
As if a bangin' rhythmic flow.

Ain't No Luv 4 a Nigga

Intent on lightin' every fire,

Set on strengthening all desires,

N return she fu%$#? another nigga,

Tried 2 add up the figures,

Presumed u would respond much bigga,

Instead u sh$% on a nigga?

Murdered me softly,

As she mentally put the gauge 2 my center,

& pulled the fu$#in' trigga.

Briitist Daye

June 12th signifies the moment,

The world was graced with your spirit,

Your smile is (quite) obviously most significant,

4 all kind & thoughtful gestures that u do,

Through & through,

Giving so much of yourself,

With a selfless attitude,

On this special day,

I wanted 2 acknowledge & give much appreciation,

Exclusively 2 u.

*Formerly Sauntia Daye

Dedicated to: the dream-killaz and all those who make it their mission to break a brotha for all that he has

The Price Ain't Rite

She was so shady,

Went and had a baby,

U were supposed to be my lady,

U were supposed to have my baby,

Eliminated the chance of even maybe,

Just like that,

You had 2 try & play me,

Left a brotha feelin' hazy,

Did u think u could phase me,

Now your tail is lookin' lazy,

Left alone cause you faulty,

In & out of relationships,

Since that foundation is shaky,

Venomous towards men,

Because of previous cats,

Whose character was excessively petty,

Later 4 that a#%,

Images of u,

Are sleazy,

Crowning flashbacks of,

Door Knob Amy

2∞

Never had a chance 2 take u on shopping sprees,

Never had a chance 2 take u on 1st class trips with me,

What a brotha got 2 do,

Do I have 2 get down on bending knees,

4 u 2 c thru the veil what your luv means,

4 u 2 c thru the veil,

The endless care & passion 4 u I bring,

4 u 2 c thru the veil,

That u r my everything.

For The First Lady - Michelle Obama & all the sisters, mothers who respect their precious selves

*Celebratin' the Queens of the Earth

Whichever way your life may lead,
There's something you must promise me,
2 never forget you're a Nubian Queen,
Always hold on to future dreams,
(I know) life ain't what it seems,
Stayin' strong isn't an easy thing,
Yet faith is a guide 4 the unseen,
No matter how much distance between,
I got your back,
From you to me,
Don't let society & others,
Define who you b,
Not only a proud Black Woman,
But a diamond in the rough,
So plain to see,
Unquestionably,
A poetic masterpiece,
There are no bounds,
To feats u can reach,
On your arrival,
A priceless jewel to the world,
Was unleashed.

*formerly called "Celebratin' Lady Love"

I Know I'm SOMEBODY...

'cause GOD don't make no JUNK!

- Unknown

Proverbial Interlude

"A greedy/vain man or woman is never content." -Unknown

"Money is the mother's milk of politics." -Unknown

"Still water runs deep." -Anonymous

"You may be right, but you may be dead right." –Anonymous
 * Enjoy today as you prepare for tomorrow.

"The fish would have never gotten captured, if he only kept his mouth shut." - The Holy Bible

"Inch by inch anything is a cinch." –Anonymous

"Leave that which makes you doubt, for that which does not make you doubt." -The Holy Quran

"Give a man some fish and he has food for the night, teach a man how to fish and he has food for a lifetime." –The Holy Bible

"If the eyes had no tears the soul would have no rainbow." – Origin, Native American proverb

"Love looks not with the eyes but with the heart." -Shakespeare

"There is no fire like passion, there is no shark like hatred, there is no snare like folly, there is no torrent like greed." -Buddha

"The wealth which enslaves the owner isn't wealth." -Yuroba

"A united family eats from the same plate." -Baganda Proverb

"You can easily determine the character of a man by how he treats those who can do nothing for him." -Malcolm Forbes

"The kingdom of heaven is within you; and whosoever shall know himself shall find it." -Egyptian Proverb

"Don't be afraid to stand for what you believe in, even if that means standing alone." -Unknown

"Life is short, live it. Love is rare, grab it. Anger is bad, dump it. Fear is awful, face it. Memories are sweet, cherish it." -Unknown

"Being happy doesn't mean that everything is perfect; it means that you've decided to look beyond the imperfections." -Unknown

"Life is like photography. You need the negatives to develop." – Unknown

"The biggest failure you can have in life is making the mistake of never trying at all." – Unknown

"Build your own dreams, or someone else will hire you to build theirs." – Farrah Gray

"A beautiful thing is never perfect." -Egyptian Proverb

"When you get to wit's end, remember that God lives there."

-Folk saying

"It is better to be hated for what you are than loved for what you are not." -Andre Gide

"What lies behind us and what lies before us are tiny matters compared to what lies within us." - Ralph Waldo Emerson

"Some people change jobs, spouses, and friends—but never think of changing themselves." - Paula Giddings

"What you do speaks so loudly that I cannot hear what you say." –Ralph Waldo Emerson

"Fear less, hope more, eat less, breathe more, talk less, say more, love more, and all good things will be yours." –Swedish Proverb

"Everything has its beauty, but not everyone sees it." -Confucius

"Noble deeds and hot baths are the best cures for depression." – Dodie Smith

"If it was meant for you to have then you will receive it, but if it was never meant for you to have then you will never obtain it." –The Holy Quran

"Tell me and I'll forget. Show me and I may not remember. Involve me and I'll understand." –Originally a Native American Proverb

"False ambition serves the neck." –Egyptian Proverb

*A true friend is worth more than twenty fair weather friends.

*Created by the author

By brother Haneef Sabree
For all intriguing minds.

FANTASY AND FICTION

The Dragon Tale

Once upon a time in the kingdom of Mountonia there lived an invincible dragon. This wasn't your ordinary creature of great fire-breathing power. For this dragon was a protector of his lands; by which rivers and streams of sustenance flow.

All those who dared to infringe and destroy his pride treasures suffered a costly lost. The dragon became known as "Drexxon." As time passed on, century after century his versatility became legendary.

THE END.

SABREEISMS

Sexelente – extremely beautiful and seductive

rawilism – the process of being realistic, void of fiction

wolfarro – a leader of great integrity and humility

folklorian – one who tells masterful stories

vegelishis – pure, untainted

re-empowerment – to restore strength, vigor, desire and confidence

terralacious – relentless, unyielding; extremely terrible

babilyhon – immature, behaving in a manner inconsistent with ones' age

lionisis – the state, by which the heart and mind are unwavering and impervious to deceit and corruption

kermetize – shell-shocked, overwhelmed psychologically

candyappliscious – very pleasing to the naked eye

textahlent – a person who sends texts disproportionately or uncontrollably

mornoon – late morning or early afternoon

psychelusto – entails a balanced/heightened awareness of the psychological and physical flesh

cognettical – mental energy

Mental Salvation

In concern of the unprincipled, I direct civilization to energize their visions of – 'what does one expect in the future.' Speaking on principles, one must know that morals and integrity are entangled. "Acts" begin with thoughts on cause and effect, wherewith negligence towards principles lead to misfortunate results.

And in this great place of our character design, one should enlist vision into the equation – adding value to their principles. It's also important to respect the positive energy that conducts morale, avoiding many setbacks that plague humanity.

Our principles are developed in a deep chamber in our hearts; a vault where love and respect will be influential throughout all levels of existence. For nature has you covered and hard work pays off.

In conclusion, don't suffer the unnecessary physical wear and tear of unprincipled stop and go compromise. On the other hand, giving others life and being a peacemaker unto the guilty who may not understand your eternal congruence is indispensable.

- Kreating Lucrative Opportunities
Author of
"Don't Call Me the N-Word"

Custom Made

2 day is all about u
A time 2 reflect on the trials & triumphs you've been thru
Your birth being a blessing is not opinion but a fact
Indubitably true
Personally I'm so glad I met u
Just make sure u continue 2 take care of self & wealth
And do what u do
Neva let any 1 define your inner view(s)
Never let any 1 or any entity discourage what u pursue
Because the world is your tool
Havin' a teacher station of ratiocination
Babygirl
The world is your school
You've persevered despite setbacks & strain
Therefore
The gem n u shall 4 eva reign
Your entrance
marked the arrival of a Queen
Inspired by Heaven's graze
Nothin' short
Of custom-made.

Fever of Luv

When I think of u,

Endless thoughts run thru my head,

Thoughts of a lova's kiss,

Thoughts of un-ending bliss,

Images of your sexy smile,

U bring out my internal wild,

No need for me to ask how,

I luv your globe & physique,

I respect what you think,

My love 4 you is permanently stained,

In my left ventricle,

With ink,

So truly is thee unique,

You electrify me baby,

singularly through,

Your anatomical suites.

If I Ever,

If I ever brought u any stress,

That was never in my plans,

If I ever disrespected your voice & mind,

Never was that my intent you will find,

If I ever caused you hurt & pain,

I pray it doesn't forever remain,

I strive to be the best man I can,

And always take a noble stand,

I know I'm not a perfect man,

You are a Princess without debate,

I envision 4 you a joyous fate,

It's quoted that life is what you make,

Never doubt your beautiful self,

From inside lies enormous wealth,

With no regrets,

I give to you my all,

Nothin' less.

Lil' Miss Cutie Pie

I always had a thing for you,
Since our days at "The High,"
I call you Lil' Miss Cutie Pie,
If I said I didn't care for you,
That would be a lie,
Don't let nothing in this world,
Make your soul cry,
If you don't do anything else 4 me,
Just make sure to keep your spirits sky high,
Persevere thru the hurt & pain,
& you will see the world with a better eye,
Events in life may lead you to question why,
U are composed of beautiful riches
That no one could ever deny,
Hold on my Queen,
Cause I know everything will turn out "fly,"
I could never change what happened in the past,
So I focus on makin' certain the same mistakes don't amass,
If I ever hurt u I apologize indeed 4 inflictin' that emotional crash,
U are 4 all time implanted in my upper left chamber mass,
In case this be my last,
For u true,
(the 1 whose lovin' can),
(make a grown man cry),
I dedicate this 2,
Lil' Miss Cutie Pie.

Mirage, My Queen

A king is nothin',

Without the complement of his Queen,

Through you I discovered so many beautiful

& wonderful things,

When I look into your regal eyez,

I see elegance & prestige,

With you I've cherished & built unforgettable

Memories,

Withstanding the trials of the thick & thin,

You've given me happiness & peace as an admirable friend,

Therefore on this Valentine's Day,

With my deepest, deepest love 4 u,

From the heart,

I send.

For Keisha

No Distance Between

If I could have written da' script,

The pic would have a different clip,

(But) I know u have 2 dip,

So I wouldn't begin to tripp',

And if you feel it's best for you,

I'm all for it too,

But damn,

I'll sho' miss u,

Promise me to take care of my Jewel,

Always movin' forward,

Is 1 of life's Golden Rules,

So no matter what it might seem,

No matter what the distance between,

Holla at me,

If in my direction,

U need 2 lean.

Dowhn4mifamilee

I blame the inept state & buffoonery,

4 breakin' my sista's heart,

2 the guilty,

A middle finger & no luv mentality,

I will impart,

Bout 2 b a lot of casualties,

Because I won't miss my mark,

Doubterz,

Can't handle me,

Str8 general 2 eternity,

Down 4 my family,

I know dem bustas, back-slayers

And as#-kissers,

Will be elated,

When there's no more life,

N Young Breed.

For Taurus

West Memphis

Shouts out 2 my homie,

West of the Mississippi,

U know what time it is,

Rep your city,

Keep on gettin' it,

I know dat' grind ain't easy,

Str8 from the "Murda Mitten,"

I greet my boy wit' da pound,

Like my souljas from Ink-Town,

Dem boyz west of Memphis,

Know how 2 get down,

To my comrade from the M-Town,

When we he hook up,

Once again it's on.

Sorri Littlle Coloured Boye

I may give u 3 to 4 times more work,

U r extremely qualified still rank u as a serf,

While your co-workers complete next to nothin'

Or take 4ever to finish a single task,

Refuse to give u a pass or advance,

Because u don't kiss any as#,

Even occasionally toss around the word nigger

During conversation,

Do u not see me standing here?

Sorri, littlle coloured boye.

I'll even murder u point blank,

And get away with it 2,

Remindin' u n the AmeriKKKas,

Your life don't mean sh%t,

"STAND YOUR GROUND"—green light 2 senselessly kill,

Regurgitated & backed,

By a Jim Crowism Floridian Act,

Our judicial system and laws of the land r fatally jacked,

Fatally whack,

No need 2 b shocked @ the "not guilty" verdict,

When u c me strut out the court room smilin',

While my extremities are "drenched n blood,"

After receiving an encore,

And voluminous pats on the back,

I'm sorri littlle coloured boye.

We know u r the most misrepresented & misquoted,
Nubian queens are the original majestics,
But somehow more than any other race of women,
R considered expendable,
& 2 frequently r disrespected,
African American kings disproportionately flood cemetery blocs & slave ships,
Unfortunately we r not going to stop it,
My affiliates r pushin' out 2 huge of a profit,
Sorri, littlle coloured boye.

I'm just too dam$ ignorant, debased & unscrupulous,
2 comprehend or acknowledge,
Coloured boyes & gurlz evolutionized and revolutionized,
This planet we call earth,
Stampin' the capital "W" n World,
Life isn't fair,
I'm so sorri littlle coloured boye.

For Caliente

What is Beautiful?

I thought about what is beautiful & many images came 2 mind,

Praying that your stresses throughout the times will b low,

Simultaneously your ambitionz, desires, dreams,

Come into fruition as they blossom,

R cultivated and grow.

Synthesizing your smile, happiness & invigoratin' your soul,

Invokes the greatest of pleasures a man can fulfill 4 his queen,

As I contemplated what beautiful is,

I concluded,

Beautiful is u.

That Ain't Gangsta

You lookin' hard,
Swear u poppin' pistols,
But I saw you in a video singin' melodies,
That ain't gangsta.

Got the nerve 2 call the next man a lame,
Contrarily wit' your fists,
Regularly u beat your girl'z brains,
Sending her str8 to the E.R.
With a black and blue eye,
Or the I.C.U.
That ain't gangsta.

Religiously getting your hair & nails done,
Or inundating the barbershop,
Spending a ton,
Sporting the latest Jordans, Versace & Gucci,
Flodgin' wit Maserati's and high price jewelry,
Yeah u got all the swag,
But your kids' heads are more nappy than a tad,
& their gear resembles some hand-me-down rags,
Character str8 rank & shallow unconscionably bad,
That ain't gangsta.

2 the bitch(es) who killed my teammate, comrade on that
November 2011 date,
U will reap what u sow,
That wasn't gangsta nigga,
U r a certified ho.

Lifzrime

Livest song by T.I. is "My Type,"
Situations ain't alrite,
Why the wicked 4eva last,
And the good disappear hella fast,
Neva understood that math,
So much wisdom my grandparents passed,
Why da' gunmen enter those schools,
& on innocent (little) children proceed 2 blast,
Whateva happen 2 vanguarding the women & community,
That elapsed.
Don't have no money,
Appointed lawyer,
Justice nullified,
Go 2 prison,
Do your time,
When u get out,
Press rewind,
Find a job,
Nigga u out your mind,
Resume and credibility n turbine,
Get caught n da' system,
Double jeopardy, double crime,
Youth troubled by reading,
They build more pens,
Recidivism on the rise,
Money pig, bangin' business,
Won't decline,
Every day hit dat grind,
Can't win 4 losin',
My life's rhyme,
Whateva I have comin' 2 me,
I walk that line.

My Main Man

You said all the right things
To keep me from this grief
So I'm puttin' this here down
For my main man Haneef
Your decisions you carefully study
Your future seems so bright
We've talked about what your name means
Remember, inclined to do right
Your parents have taught you well
At no expense did they spare
The Larry Bird move, The Jordan turn around
Yeah, you mastered those there
The torch is passed to you my man
Watch over our little soldiers
Hassan, Jacque, Lee and the rest
Check them as they grow older
I'm sure you'll teach them Truth

Be sure to include its fights
Prepare them to perform extremely well
Especially when they're not in your sight
I only ask this of you
'Cause I know in my heart you can
Keep your Faith in Allah
To Haneef: my main man

-By Abdul-Kareem (Ahk)

For my cousin: Hilton Jones

Hilton's Palace

They say my cousin was a cool cat,

But now I'll never know,

Some nothin' azz niggas stole his life,

Twisted motives,

Snatched something priceless,

Should have just simply taken the dough,

Consequently there won't b any exchangin' of laughs,

As our camaraderie grows & grows.

I hear he was a giving man,

Wouldn't hesitate to lend his hand,

And help someone n need,

I know revenge is 4 the Lord,

But my eyez r filled with crimson rage,

Unable to blocc out thoughts,

Of making his killers bleed and bleed,

If they were desperate for money or material gains,

U already took his car,

Why not just pillage the bread 2?

Instead u ended my cousin's life.

Police have no suspects,

Can't depend on them 4 shi%,

Let u cruise down the Ave or Jefferson with tinted windows thou,

Or a rolling stop (that) u commit,

Robocop and Pacman will b on that azz hella swift,

I envision him in a better place,

N a palace 4ever he will reside,

To my big cuz,

I'll keep fightin' the good fight 4 u homie,

Until we meet on the other side.

Intangibles

Distinguished Establishments
(Inkster, MI area)

- Soulfood to Go – Sister Saniyyah
- Bubba's Barbershop
- Marcel's Beauty Salon/Barbershop
- Pearson's Insurance Company
- Big 4 Cab Company – Brother Ibrahim (Heem)
- Knox Restaurant & Catering
- Cutz Lounge (Coming Soon) – Mr. Williams
- Bishop Auto Wrecking
- Lloyd Holt Auto Storage
- Japaree Beauty Supply – Mr. Day
- Cannon's Warehouse
- D-Dees Farmers Market
- K's Wing Station (Mr. Ulmer)

Music & Movie Classicz

Music
- Shell Shocked – Mac
- World War III – Mac
- Nycewitit – Nycewitit
- Reality Check – Seagram
- The Martyr – Immortal Technique
- Made – Scarface
- The Best of Sam Cooke – Sam Cooke
- Love Deluxe – Sade
- I Am Legend Mixxx Tape – Pone
- Coming Soon… - AO

Movies
- The Longshots – Ice Cube
- Hidden Colors I & II
- Bloods & Crips: Made In America
- Welcome to Death Row
- The Greatest – Muhammad Ali
- Posse
- Panther
- Tupac: Resurrection

Sitcoms & Recommended Websites

Sitcoms
- What's Happening
- Martin
- A Different World
- Moesha
- Living Single
- Knight Rider
- The Fresh Prince of Bel-Air
- 21 Jump Street
- New York Undercover
- Three's Company

Websites
- www.golfwearandmore.com
- www.hjsabree.wix.com/jrhandsonsllc
- www.hjsabree.wix.com/young-breed-productions
- www.hsabree1.organogold.com

Reading List

- Don't Call Me the N-Word – Kreating Lucrative Opportunities
- It Can Happen to You: Vol. 1 – Phette Ogburn
- Vernon the Vegetable Man – Yvelette Stines
- Trumping a Fixed Deck – Haneef Sabree
- Hidden Truth – Sherry Weaver
- Ventricular Soliloquies – Haneef Sabree
- Readings about the "Black Wall Street" in Tulsa Oklahoma
- Lies My Teacher Told Me – James W. Loewen
- Making the Impossible Possible – Bill Strickland
- Love – Toni Morrison

Bonus: Compliments to my Supporters

For: Dack, Pokie, Naeem, Reginal, Marvin Lee, Eric & Art

Buster Free

Suckers try to pull my card,

But I leave them stankin', wrinkled, & charred,

I have to get my ends,

No I don't have a phat Benz,

It doesn't even matter thou,

Cause I keep my profile tight,

Like an optical lens,

You can trip if you want to,

But in the end,

I'll be the victor,

Not you.

Dancinawfbeet

I'm outdee 5 thowl,

Imitators couldn't mimic my style,

It's too buck wild,

Got em' askin',

"can I jock now?"

Consistently got the flavor pumpin',

Outlastin' the parameters of a mile,

As that cool cat Slimm,

Don't tripp off da' techneek,

Dudes swear they supa stars,

Can't even compete,

Their words so bleak,

Females layin' & layin',

Chasin' dem treats,

Stunnas' keep playin',

Neva learnin',

Til' they knocked off they feet,

Tryin' to reach that level,

Searchin' everywhere else (on earth),

But inside of me,

Still dancing off beat,

Why that be,

akhee?

The Reboh

Keeps the ground stable beneath his/her feet,

Never displays signs of being weak or meek,

If a situation pops off,

Is ready to compete,

Exhibits no fear,

Even when death is near,

Speaks whatever is on the mind,

Instead of simply chuckling and accepting a lie,

One in which the government truly hates,

Cause a reboh will do all it takes,

Going against the deceptive & oppressive laws politicians make,

Despite his/her life being at stake.

21 Gun Salute

Medals of Honor

- Hilton Jones
- Stanley Brown
- Coach Warren Woods
- Gloria Scribbling
- Tremaine Pool
- Allen Willis
- Phillip Pernell (H.S. teammate)
- Milton (H.S. teammate)
- Russell (Lexington Pky.)
- Uncle Thomas Harrison
- Ira Harrison
- Marvin Harrison
- Mrs. Gertie Inman
- Mr. Julius Inman
- Mr. Arthur Watts
- Mrs. Howard
- Mr. Simmons
- Mr. Anderson aka Mr. A (Dorm Director @ PSC)
- Coach Parker

Acknowledgments

My Parents - The Sabrees, Christina, Leslie, Naim Tha Dream, Rhonda, Sonia Peterson, Kinda Hunter, The Masons, Bro. Gary Al-Kasib- The Al-Kasibs, Jihads, Mike Wright, Ken Overman- The Overmans, Sis. Rafia Muhammad, Ben Coats Jr., Alex Lozon, Wendell & Kevin Ulmer – The Ulmers, Keisha Hamby, Renee Inman, Shana Oglesby, Yvelette Stines, Oscar Grant III, The Sharriefs, Shanae Williams, Marissa Alexander, The Urban Network Bookstore/Café, Spectacles in Harmony Park, Shrine of the Black Madonna, Can You Picture This Inc., The Crazy Wisdom Bookstore, United Sonz and everyone who has supported my ambitions, thank you.

Topic: Field Studies & Life Skill Development

Problem: Students are deficient of basic life skills, concept of action versus consequences, and age appropriate self-control

Variables: First-Hand Visuals

Game Plan/Solutions

Organize trips where students witness first-hand the process and results of actions versus consequences. Dialogue afterwards with students is encouraged to create a more engaged learning environment. The following solutions will promote students to think more critically and rationally. Furthermore, these recommendations have been proven to be effective if implemented sufficiently.

Recommended Locations

1) Court House – Watch an actual court proceeding. Ex. Cases involving DUI (Driving Under the influence), B & E (breaking & entering), robbery, drugs, homicide, etc.
B) Students are given a tour of the jail facility. They are directed to step inside the cell and look around
2) Teen Health Center – Students are exposed to the realities of childcare, child abortions, and the non-glamorous aspects tied to poor decision making
3) The Morgue – A picture is worth a thousand words
• Students can visually see the dangers of actions without thinking/thought, unhealthy associations, and making ill-advised choices

4) ER (Emergency Room) – Educated regarding the horrors of gun play, getting caught in the wrong place at the wrong time, or emotionally charged immaturity. E.g. head trauma injuries from gunshot victims, overdose incidents, injuries from drunk driving, and so on.

*Concluding Points

The youth, students are non-responsive (by in large), regarding one-to-one conferences, pep talks, and verbal redirection. The students' mentalities are they have to touch the fire to realize or believe that the fire is hot. This sort of misguided thinking produces a volatile, destructive road to travel on.

Primary Reference:The teachings of Dr. Jawanza Kunjufu

Thank you, Mr. Sabree

Proposed Initiative Part I

Statement of the Problem
An unfavorable percentage of students are below a satisfactory level in applying basic operations and cognizance with the time tables.

Methods for Doing the Work/Solutions
Constant: Competition
Variable(s): Manipulative Use

Time Table Initiative

1) Weekly time table quiz bowl: one team versus another (time tables 0-12s) e.g. girls versus boys, members of the track team versus members of the basketball team, etc.

   **Note:
   - Higher level learners can work directly with lower level learners, serving as junior teachers in the classroom
   - Brain teaser activities such as kakuro (strongly suggested) and suduku puzzles or math detective exercises can be issued to accelerated learners. (Math detective exercises contain riddles and story problems that must be mathematically figured out in order to solve the case/mystery)

Rewards:

The team with the most wins at the end of the card marking will receive a prize, ex. bag with snacks/supplies (cereal/granola bars, fruit snacks, pencils, pens, and/or ribbon/certificate. (Groups no larger than approximately 6 - 8)

2) Students pair up with one another and utilize flash cards to test time table comprehension, (simulating the card game "War" for example). No more than three students per group – management purposes. This second suggestion can be substituted in for Bell Work- approximately a 15 minute exercise.

3) Students create a multiplication table booklet. The booklet should include: an artistic cover/back page, time tables 0-12, interests, hobbies, at least one paragraph regarding three or more aspirations in life, etc. The former addresses the anticipatory set.

Applying Basic Operations – fractions, computations

1. Utilize Games: Monopoly and Money Bingo. (Groups ranging in number from 4 – 6)

    a) Monopoly: students are prompted to apply and gain practice with the four basic operations via the use of money. Also, addresses the development of communication, social, money management, and thinking skills.

Procedures:

1) Instructor explains the process and guidelines of the game to the class. Then the teacher answers any questions or concerns by the students. Furthermore, a brief inquiry phase can take place to evaluate how well the students retained the information.

2) The class is split into groups so that a balance exists between higher and lower level learners. The group leaders in the class could be given the responsibility of arranging the groups, (occasionally).

3) The students begin playing the game based on the instructions provided and the details of the game explained by the instructor. Group leaders can assign the responsibilities & duties: ex. Banker and realtor (student handling the property).

4) For assessment purposes the facilitator should navigate around the room taking mental notes and asking questions periodically.

- Teachers are urged to monitor student behavior throughout the activity.

5) To obtain satisfactory results, the groups may need adjusting or rearranging from time to time.

6) Incentives are suggested at the discretion of the teacher—applying creativity is recommended.

> **b) Money/Math Bingo:** students practice and improve their comprehension of the basic operations and number sense through money/coins; furnishes a means to build social and communication skills as well.

Procedures:

1) Instructor will explain to the class the process and guidelines for the bingo activity. After providing an explanation, the floor is made available to any questions the students may have. A short inquiry phase could be put in place to evaluate how well the students retained the explanation about the game play.

2) The class is split into groups, (no more than 4 - 6 students per group). Each group is formulated based on the skill level of the learner. Some of the more responsible students could be in charge of setting up the groups on occasion.

3) The students play the money bingo game according to the rules set forth in the instructions and the guidelines expressed by the facilitator.

4) Instructor is encouraged to walk around the class taking mental notes and periodically asking questions. (assessment step)

- Monitoring student behavior/conduct throughout the activity is important.

5) Facilitator may need to adjust groups from time to time in order to achieve acceptable performance results.

6) Incentives may be issued at the discretion of the teacher—innovativeness is recommended.

2. Measurement – (focuses on fractions)

　　a) students make predictions on the perimeter and area of at least 5 objects

　　b) create a table to record the predictions for perimeter and area, the actual measurements and the objects chosen

　　c) use a measuring tape (preferred/practical) or ruler to determine the actual measurements in centimeters, millimeters, and inches

　　d) record the data

　　e) summarize how your predictions stacked up against the actual measurements (at least a paragraph)

　　f) explain the problems you experienced and how you resolved them

　　g) what you learned from the measurement activity is described with detail

*Duration: Twice a month (at least)

Expected Results

Improvements in the stated problem areas are anticipated.

Proposed Initiative Part II

Statement of Problem
Students are not completing their homework. Overall, they're not putting forth the effort required to simply fulfill their homework responsibilities.

Methods for Doing the Work/Solutions
Constant: Competition
Variable: N/A

> 1) Have a special meeting at least three times a year. Parties involved: parents, teachers, students, and positive people.
>
> Purpose: re-emphasize face-to-face the necessity for students to complete their homework
>
> Note: Select teachers per grade level to conduct the meeting in separate rooms. This is suggested to prevent poor ratios between the teachers and concerned attendees.
>
> 2) *Competitive Edge*
>
> - Each class: young ladies versus the young men regarding completing homework assignments. Winners receive some sort of incentive, (duration could start at one week then steadily progress to a month and eventually a card marking).
>
> - **inner grade level** battles: e.g. one sixth grade class versus another sixth grade class
>
> - **school-wide:** Have the competition posted in a conspicuous manner for everyone to see, (location – hallway). Battles between different grade levels occur for the entire school:
> **Rewards** - class with the best homework rating will earn a sharp leadership trophy. The runner-up class will inherit a "pride certificate."

3) 10% deduction minimum, towards overall grade for failing homework requirements, ex. B transforms into a C. (this policy is consistent throughout the school)

*Note: deductions are not to exceed 15 – 20 %. A memo is sent home to parents at the beginning and middle of the school year, (as a reminder).

Expected Results
1) The performance level of the students in reference to homework, should noticeably increase

Note: It's critical that the students receive both short and long term rewards throughout the process

Words of Wisdom

I AM AN IDEA

CONCEIVED IN THE MIND OF THE UNIVERSE

AND INTERPRETED IN THE MINDS

OF THE INDIVIDUALS I MEET

WITHIN MYSELF I AM CONSTANT

YET I AM AS EVER CHANGING

AS THE PEOPLE WHO INTERPRET ME

I CAN CONTROL MY ACTIONS

BUT I CAN NOT CONTROL THEIR THOUGHTS

THEREFORE, I MUST DO WHAT I THINK RIGHT

AND LET OTHERS-

THINK WHAT THEY WILL.

-Unknown

Soliloquies by
Bro. Dennis Sabree
Aka "The Truth"

Why do you have to go?

Have I waited too late?

Who is calling in the night?

What compelling force beckons

You from afar?

Boredom destroys the mind,

The body, and the spirit.

Boredom eats at the

Vital tissues of life.

Maybe next time,

Yea, maybe next time.

Upon first glance those mountains
Scrape the sky.
While approaching their awesomeness
Tranced my every thought.
From seemingly the abyss, I stood
In sheer amazement.

Loss of a dear friend often strips
The vulnerable tendons of mental
Stamina.
Death to a loved one or kin solicits
Profound thoughts and, perhaps,
Scarlet rainbows.
Elimination of Life's work tends to
Maim.

Yet, aint no mountain high enough,
And with each pulsation, however,
Faint there is Life.

No more talking at people,
Work has ended with people,
Retired smiles for people,
At last no more people;

Years since being with you,
A week craving for you,
All day thinking of you,
At last alone with you;

Boisterous streets are muzzled,
At last two hearts are muzzled;

Ah, finally the time has come,
Too late, gone, At last.

I'm a factory worker,……………………….. nigguh!

I am a doctor,……………………………………..nigguh!

I'm an electrician,……………………………….nigguh!

I'm a pimp,………………………………………….nigguh!

I am a minister,…………………………………..nigguh!

Nigguh, nigguh, nigguh, nigguh,………………………..!

I'm a black man and having had my jewels ripped off from my shi$, my mind is no longer universal, no longer American, no longer negro, but to its infinitesimal crevices cold black.

Who is it that loves meat?

Who is sometimes found with long hair

And other times with short hair?

Who, when annoyed twitches incessantly

Until tranquility is restored?

Who is it, upon which Mother Nature can place no boundary?

Who uses every attribute possessed to survive?

Who has watched members of his family coerced into domestication?

And after deliberating his condition does not roar before killing; who?

This day I met a most attractive girl.
By chance, my life altered during a talk.
Each time my thoughts conjure simply a pearl.
Perhaps, tonight a rendezvous, a walk.

Ebony rich her hair, designed it not.
Thoughtful, but more fragile, gleeful her eyes
The face tinted mostly by time than lot.
Modest shoulders, soft breast, loins fine size.

Light weight surely, on an intellect scale,
Certainly not deterred simply by trends.
For sure, life molds her thoughts as not to fail.
One mind from two as interweaving mends.

Many cry out; "too young," to be her beau!
To them, I scream, softly of course, not so.

"Nothing is more powerful and liberating than knowledge."
—William H. Gray III

"Africa is herself a mother. The mother of mankind."
—Maya Angelou

"Jazz is the nobility of the race put into sound." —Wynton Marsalis
"Small details of your lives are what really matter in a relationship."
—Unknown

"Find time to be your significant other's or spouse's friend and do those little things for each other that build intimacy."
-Anonymous

*Answer to the question from the beginning of the book:

So that you will listen twice as much as you talk.

Empty The Whole Clip

HANEEF SABREE
your City Councilman for District 2

I am running for City Council because I believe in restoring power to the people

As a longtime resident, educator, and mentor of Inkster my VISION is to:
- Genuinely address and be proactive regarding the concerns and plight of the community, especially the young adults
- Create safer streets and reduce the occurrence of violence in our neighborhoods
- Provide better accommodations for the senior citizens
- Increase community employment
- Support our local block clubs
- Increase revenue in the city, by which the Inkster residents are the primary beneficiaries
- Support the growth of a greater percentage of businesses owned by Inkster residents

CARDINAL OBJECTIVES
- Serve as an example of sound principles and integrity
- Improving the overall productivity of the community
- Motivating and establishing a strong foundation for the young
- Making a positive difference
- Leading by example and actions not false promises and lip service
- Resonant the voice of the people

Credentials: Inkster High Graduate, 1996 Salutatorian, Philander Smith College, Bachelors of Science 2002, Marygrove College, Masters of Education 2009, Teacher Certification K-8, Assistant Coach Inkster High Freshmen Boys Basketball 2007-2008

*Supported/endorsed by the UAW
*Volunteers are welcome!

Paid for by The Committee to Elect Haneef Sabree
(Inkster Primary Election 2011)

For: Darren Reeves

My Brother D

From childhood I've looked up 2 my brother D,

There's not 2 much more important than 1s family,

Advice, wisdom or laughter he provided that with consistency,

Direction, dependability and authenticity,

Were all a relevancy,

Gifted me with my first & only canine, Tuff, I could call my

Very own,

Used to take me 2 my games @ St. Cecilia's in da "D",

Back then man,

I was makin' catz feel me,

Cause I was n a zone,

Cannot 4get the magic,

He had such an impact,

An original soulja,

That's my brother D.

Dedicated to: single mothers, single fathers, mothers, fathers & all those who bust their tail on a regular, to give their children the best this world has to offer and everything they never had.

That's My D.O.A.E.D.D².I.

Doesn't receive the props he deserves,

Published remarkable editorials with no preserves,

That's my d.o.a.e.d.d².i.

He taught me how to swim & ride a bike,

Mentally prepared me so I could soar as a kite,

That's my d.o.a.e.d.d².i.

Through his actions I know with resolution,

I don't need anyone's approval to feel loved,

& if a man hits, whips or abuses me,

The worse form of this is emotionally & mentally,

He's not a man,

He is lower than scum,

That's my d.o.a.e.d.d².i.

Served as an example of a man equated to responsibility

And accountability,

Not physical prowess, status, deep pockets nor sexual expertise,

That's my d.o.a.e.d.d².i.

Words to live by,

I can hear him speak,

Treat that woman/man with the utmost respect,

Give her/him 100,

Until there's nothin' left,

Keep the ground steady beneath the feet,

All that is trivial will become obsolete,

He rendered everything I needed 2 become an honorable woman or man,

Lest u forget,

Encompassin' but not limited 2,

Eye contact, preservation of dignity and a strong sturdy hand,

He made some mistakes,

But he was always there when I needed him,

His M.O. was just do the best that u can,

My gratitude goes out 2 u,

Because that's my d.o.a.e.d.d^2.i.

*his/her, he/she, him/her (correct pronoun usage determined by if referring to the mother or the father)

(F) Haneef Sabree #32, (B) Leon Bouldin #22: "Taking It 2 the Rack"
1994- 1995 Inkster Varsity Basketball Season – Da' High Til I Die

Ever Ask Why – Unreleased

Why do a large number of Whites think I'm a nigger

Why do so many Blacks try to burn me like a cinder

Why they get animalistic on Emmitt Till

What's up wit Chaldeans shootin' and bashin' brothas wit tire irons for a thrill

Hispanics & Middle-easterners r cool wit romancin' black women

Flip the script

& they want 2 chop me up like a scene from Kill Bill

Every figure out why da' Chinaman stays on ill

Why r insurance companies so cannibalistic as they

Prey on the young & old collimate 2 Jack & Jill

Why as long as it doesn't concern them they say chill

Why my comrade Pac get his cap peeled

& how come no one pursued the car wit the shooter(s) on da real

Explain how brothas clashing n da street = blood distilled

What made Marvin Gaye's father take his only son with a kill

Why every time u down that alcohol u break a governmental seal

How did God get replaced by Ms. Cocaine & Mr. Pill --their kids' lust & dollar bill

Why just about every ethnicity includin' my own have 2 serve a nigga such a raw deal

DWB is a blatant form of racism cheaper than a McDonald's value meal

Why cats don't think no more str8 programmed as if a PC or microfilm

But my words u don't feel

Tell me

Why life have to be this way

Where great martyrs such as Malcolm X, Martin & Medgar

Get conspired upon and murdered thru COINTELPRO, FBI & the CIA

How come I can't find peace when I rest

Why America have to run around the world with a poked out chest

Why is my best unable to pass society's tests

When will Blacks stop allowing religion to cause so much divisive stress

How come sistas and brothas can't avoid the unnecessary friction

Since our ancestors the Egyptians represented the utmost in unified precision

How did the world end up in such a crazy disposition

To the point where despicables/sickos just up and violate our children

Why situations got my people in such an awkward position

What the hell is going on with all the gay renditions

How can I end all the head on collisions

Why the real criminals start within the governmental system

Do you really like what you see in the mirror

Is the image any clearer

Be cautious of the mirages

Fostered by (none other than)

The daily news and the media

Sellin' gimmicks and false pretenses

Like www.expedia.

Dedicated to: The General Pac

Gone But Not Forgotten - Unreleased

Foreshadowed by brotha Malcolm, George Jackson and Fred Hampton
Courtesy of the Bureau
They assassinated my hero

Claimed it was a random hit
Ain't that some sh#t
Puffy, Suge Knight & Jigga
U looney tunes r a trip,
Your hands r 4ever dirty niggas
There's no denying it—not 1 bit
Showcased gross negligence & a disregard for procedures

With no concern for the culprits
The case has implications of law enforcement
Officials involvement written all over it

Resulting in the scene being condensed & clouded
He motivated & spear-headed programs for the youth
Disseminated knowledge and exposed the truth

U had 2 feel
That fire, soul and trill
As he integrated charisma and flair
But it was that delivery

In which u could not compare
Utterances directly touched
Those whose sentiments are
Usually overlooked or abused

Those pantaloons got the game confused
I'm going to bump your music til' I die
Because that's how souljas do

In The Event of My Demise

In the event of my demise

When my heart can beat no more

I hope I die for a principle

Or a belief that I had lived 4

I will die before my time

Because I feel the shadow's depth

So much I wanted 2 accomplish

Before I reached my death

I have come 2 grips with the possibility

And wiped the last tear from my eyes

I loved all who were positive

In the event of my demise!

-Tupac Amaru Shakur

…..MARISSA ALEXANDER……………………….………..…….……

………………..OSCAR GRANT III…………REMEMBER……….………..

………………………….…THOSE NAMES……………….……..…………..

…..."INJUSTICE ANYWHERE IS A THREAT………………....…………..

………………..TO JUSTICE EVERYWHERE"…………………….……….

………………"AN UNJUST LAW IS NO LAW AT ALL"……….…………..

……...."SEEK KNOWLEDGE FROM THE WOMB TO THE TOMB"……

…………………."SEEK KNOWLEDGE FROM THE WOMB……………

TO THE TOMB"………………………………………….………………….

www.ingramcontent.com/pod-product-compliance
Lightning Source LLC
Chambersburg PA
CBHW072102290426
44110CB00014B/1787